Nelson Wilmarth Aldrich

The tariff act of 1890 defended

A speech of Nelson W. Aldrich

Nelson Wilmarth Aldrich

The tariff act of 1890 defended
A speech of Nelson W. Aldrich

ISBN/EAN: 9783744722926

Printed in Europe, USA, Canada, Australia, Japan

Cover: Foto ©ninafisch / pixelio.de

More available books at **www.hansebooks.com**

THE TARIFF ACT OF 1890 DEFENDED.

SPEECH

OF

NELSON W. ALDRICH,

OF RHODE ISLAND,

IN THE

SENATE OF THE UNITED STATES,

TUESDAY, JULY 26, 1892.

WASHINGTON.
1892.

SPEECH

OF

HON. NELSON W. ALDRICH.

The Senate having under consideration the resolution submitted by Mr. HALE, June 27, 1892, directing the Committee on Finance to inquire into the effect of a policy of "tariff for revenue only" upon the labor and industries of the United States—

Mr. ALDRICH said:

Mr. PRESIDENT: It is evident that the tariff question is to become, by common consent, the leading issue in the approaching Presidential campaign. The radical declarations of the Democratic platform adopted at Chicago, and the equally radical utterances of leading representatives of the party, insure this result.

At no time in the history of the country have the lines between the two great parties upon this question been so clearly defined. The party platforms of 1892 declare with much greater candor than is customary in papers of this kind the doctrines of their respective parties. The Republicans enter the campaign distinctively favoring the continuance of the protective policy, and announcing definitely the principles which should control tariff legislation, while, on the other hand, the Democrats denounce protection as a fraud, declare the unconstitutionality of protective tariff duties, and make a special and vicious attack upon the tariff act of 1890 as the culminating atrocity of tariff legislation.

The Democratic platform is in many respects a radical departure from any of the previous official utterances of the party. At no time in the history of the country, except in the course of the movement for nullification, has any attempt heretofore been made to make the doctrine of the unconstitutionality of protective duties the essential element of a political creed. The steps by which the Democracy have reached the radical position they now occupy have been very gradual. The Democratic platforms of 1884 and 1888 were so constructed as to secure the approval of a large

2

number of incidental protectionists who then held a place, nomi-
nally, at least, in the Democratic ranks; but in the platform of
1892 all disguises are thrown off and for the first time the party
is arrayed in emphatic antagonism to tariff rates which contain
any element of protection.

This clear alignment of parties greatly simplifies the discussion of the question. It removes all opportunity for possible
differences of opinion in regard to the Republican plan of campaign. The friends of protection must wage aggressive warfare
upon the revolutionary doctrines which, although long secretly
cherished by Democratic leaders, are now for the first time
openly avowed. The attack upon the indefensible Democratic
position must be vigorous and persistent.

I regret that a purpose to confine my remarks to-day to an examination of Democratic criticisms and attacks upon the tariff
act of 1890 precludes me from entering this attractive field. I
shall not, on the other hand, attempt to-day any general defense
of the Republican policy of protection. The progress which the
country has made under its beneficent influences during the
past thirty years furnishes the best proof of the wisdom shown
in its adoption and retention as a national policy.

Before entering upon a defense of the act of 1890, however, I
will say that the framers and supporters of this measure have
never claimed that it was perfect in all of its details; but notwithstanding this limitation, which, I infer, must be applied to
all legislative enactments covering so wide a field, I believe that
all protectionists are willing to accept the measure as a successful embodiment of Republican principles and to have the wisdom
of the policy they advocate adjudged by its practical results.

The tariff plank of the Chicago platform formulates the Democratic declaration of faith; but it has been left to the Senator
from Missouri [Mr. VEST], who seems to be the acknowledged
representative of his party in this Chamber in all matters per-
taining to tariff legislation, to announce in detail the Democratic
programme. That Senator has been zealous at all times in the
advocacy of tariff reform, and his eloquence and ability in the
treatment of the subject have made him one of the most con-
spicuous champions of the cause.

727

His acknowledged leadership, however, in this regard has never been quite so marked as at this session of Congress. If any other Senators on the opposite side of the Chamber have views upon this subject th ey have not declared them to the public.

With an intrepidity and ability worthy of a better cause, the distinguished Senator has singly and alone upheld the free-trade standard of his party

In view of this condition of affairs I shall assume that the two rather remarkable speeches made by that Senator in the Senate on the 6th and 28th of June fairly represent the line of argument which is to be followed by his party in the political campaign upon which we are about to enter.

As I shall have occasion to criticise severely most of the statements contained in these speeches, I am bound to say in advance that I do not think the distinguished Senator can be fairly held responsible for their frequent and alarming inaccuracies. The honorable Senator has undoubtedly in his great zeal allowed himself to be misled by designing and interested parties, who have sought to use his great reputation and high character to give the weight of authority to their own absurd attempts to further mislead and deceive the American people. Most of these attempts at deception are so transparent, and their inaccuracies are so grotesquely absurd that they would not be worthy of notice if it had not become evident that they were to be given a wide circulation in the approaching campai gn upon the authority of my distinguished friend.

The principal objection made by the Senator from Missouri to the tariff act of 1890 is that which was urged with great force and effect in the political campaign which immediately followed its enactment, namely, that through a large advance in rates it had effected a considerable increase in the prices of the necessaries of life and greatly augmented the cost of living of all classes of people, especially of the poor.

In his speech of June 28, page 6177 of the RECORD, the Senator from Missouri makes the following plain and unequivocal statement:

I am prepared to show that the McKinley act has had the effect of increasing prices upon the necessaries of life to the people of this country, and that
727

the statement in his resolution [referring to the Senator from Maine] that an area of cheapness in the necessaries of life is being brought to the people of the United States is absolutely and unconditionally false.

One of the principal purposes of the tariff inquiry ordered by the Senate resolution of March 3, 1891, was to ascertain with accuracy whether this claim of the opponents of protection was justified by the actual results. An investigation into the course of prices and cost of living, much more extensive and thorough than was ever before attempted, was instituted. The committee determined to ascertain the relative prices paid by actual consumers for all articles of general consumption at retail in every part of the United States on the first of each month from June, 1889, to September, 1891. This embraced a period of seventeen months prior to the passage of the act of 1890 and eleven months subsequent to that date. The quotations were in all cases secured from actual sales, taken from the books of merchants in seventy different cities and towns in the different States and Territories. The places at which quotations were obtained were selected with the view of covering the entire country geographically, and included typical commercial, manufacturing, and agricultural communities. The prices were secured by the trained experts of the Department of Labor with the greatest care.

The list of two hundred and fifteen articles on which monthly prices were thus obtained was carefully selected by the unanimous action of the committee, with a view of co vering every possible expenditure of a family in the average condition of life, that is with an income of $500 to $1,000 per annum.

The results of this comprehensive and exhaustive inquiry are contained in the report recently made by the Finance Committee. This report covers 2,300 printed pages and contains more than 1,200,000 different quotations.

The inquiry was thoroughly nonpartisan, and every possible care was taken to give to it a character which would entitle the results secured to the highest weight of authority. This investigation clearly establishes the fact that a decline instead of an advance has taken place in the prices of the necessaries of life and the resulting cost of living since the adoption of the act of 1890.

727

The articles on which prices were obtained were divided into the following groups:

1. Food.
2. Cloths and clothing.
3. Fuel and lighting.
4. House furnishing goods.
5. Drugs and chemicals.
6. Metals and and implements.
7. Lumber and building materials.

The percentage of decline in the various groups embraced in the schedule is shown by the following table, prices for June, July, and August, 1889, being taken as a basis for comparison and represented by the number 100, changes being shown by percentages of that number:

Group.

Food	100.53
Cloths and clothing	99.65
Fuel and lighting	98.69
Metals and implements	97.49
Lumber and building materials	98.28
Drugs and chemicals	95.96
House-furnishing goods	99.83
Miscellaneous	100.52
Average	99.36

The Finance Committee also investigated for the same period the course of wholesale prices at the great distributing centers. While this investigation disclosed greater fluctuations in price of the articles selected, the general result was the same, the fall in wholesale prices running substantially parallel with that of retail prices.

It will be observed that the greater percentages of decline are in the groups of manufactured articles, where it was claimed the greatest advance had taken place.

In addition to the inquiry stated above, the committee caused retail prices of the different articles included in these lists to be taken on May 1, 1892, at three of the points at which the original inquiry was made, namely, Fall River, Mass., Chicago, Ill., and Dubuque, Iowa. The result of this latter inquiry shows that a still further decline in prices and in the cost of living had taken place between September 1, 1891, and May 1, 1892, clearly establishing a continuance of the tendency to lower prices and lower cost of living.

727

It is shown as a net result of the investigation that prices and the cost of living, based on the expenditures of a family in ordinary circumstances, had declined 3.4 per cent in May, 1892, as compared with the period prior to the adoption of the tariff act of 1890.

It is difficult to see how the results of this thoroughly exhaust-ive inquiry could be a surprise to anyone, unless he should be a professional tariff reformer. It has, I believe, been for many months apparent to the great mass of the people of the United States that none of the Democratic predictions in regard to higher prices and greater cost of living, as the result of the tariff legislation of 1890, had been fulfilled.

There can be no longer any question as to the course of prices for the period covered by the committee's investigation. Even the Democratic platform, which undertakes to enumerate the evil effects of the act of 1890, abandons the claim that its adoption resulted in increased prices, and I am greatly surprised to find that the cry is now being revived for the campaign of 1892. I do not believe it is possible, however, for the same men to deceive the American people twice with the same misstatements in regard to the same subject, especially when the second attempt is made after the facts have been ascertained and are well known to the people of the country. The allegations made in regard to prices in October, 1890, were then made with such vehemence and pertinacity that many honest men were deluded. This experience can not, in my opinion, be repeated.

It is true that the percentages of decline of prices and cost of living and the advance in wages, as shown by the report, are not large. Movements of this kind, from the nature of the case, are always slow. The price of a single article or even a group of articless may change greatly, or the wages in a single occupation or group of occupations may advance or decline rapidly, and still the average of all the great mass of prices or wages not be changed perceptibly. A slight change in the total average, however, makes a great difference in the aggregate result. The decline in the cost of living from June, 1889, to May, 1892, as shown by the report of the Finance Committee, was 3.4 per cent. The advance in wages, as shown by the same report, was .75 of 1 per cent. This makes an average advance in the purchasing power of wages of 4.15 per cent. Assuming $600 as the average income of the families of the country, this would be equivalent to, say, $25 per family, or an aggregate saving for 13,000,000 families of $325,-000,000 for each year.

The addition of this vast sum annually to the national earnings and wealth is an achievement which speaks with a more eloquent voice than I can command in behalf of a policy under which such results are possible.

It is very significant that while the cost of living in the United States declined for the period covered by the investigation of the Finance Committee, the cost of living in England increased 1.9 per cent. If the conditions had been reversed, our Democratic friends would have insisted that this was the direct and logical result of rival revenue systems. I am curious to see what explanation they will now make. The result is unquestionably a very surprising one to them, and one which they will have difficulty in explaining away. While the attempt to compare average retail prices in England and the United States is not satisfactory, I am convinced that for a family buying the same quantity and quality of articles at retail in the two countries, that the cost of living would not be higher in America. These relative conditions. however, do not exist, as the scale of living for the masses of people in the respective countries is vastly different.

At no time in our history have the earnings of the American people been as great, measured by their power to purchase the comforts and necessaries of life, as they are to-day. Measured by the same standard they are vastly greater than those of any other people in the world.

The Senator from Missouri based his broad statement, so strikingly at variance with understood facts, that the recent tariff act has increased the prices of the necessaries of life, on two statements which he submitted, with every appearance of confidence, and to which he was kind enough to invite my special attention. The first of these was a table prepared by Mr. Daniel McKeever, of the importing house of H. Herman Sternbach & Co., of New York, purporting to show the relative cost to import twenty-one articles before and after the passage of the act of 1890. As the articles named in Mr. McKeever's list were selected by that gentleman from the very large number of imported articles that go into consumption, for the purpose of showing a general advance in prices, his compilation is deserving of notice.

It is evident from the language used by the Senator from Missouri in reference to this table that he was willing to rest his case upon the accuracy of its representations. It will be noticed, however, that Mr. McKeever does not claim that the cost of the articles named had been increased to consumers. It is evident, however, that the Senator from Missouri intended to create the impression, both by his language and his triumphant manner, that the paper would in some manner prove beyond all question that a general advance in the price of the necessaries of life had taken place.

Under these circumstances I feel justified in making an examination of the document, which otherwise I should pass by unnoticed, as entirely unimportant and irrelevant to the question at issue as to the effect of the tariff act of 1890. The table purports to show the relative foreign cost in New York, duty paid, of the articles named therein, of which samples were exhibited, before and after October, 1890, the relative rates of duty assessed by existing law and the equivalent ad valorem rate; and the duties in force prior to the date the act of 1890 went into effect.

I will first ask your attention to the statement of relative rates of duties. I assume that it was Mr. McKeever's intention, as it certainly was that of the Senator from Missouri, to create the inference that the increase of rates shown in the table furnishes a fair indication of the character of the general changes in rates effected by the act of 1890. I believe I shall be able to show that the statement has no value for this purpose. Such of its comparisons as are not grossly inaccurate are wholly misleading. For instance, Mr. McKeever states that the rates upon astrachans, samples 18, 19, 20, and 21, prior to the act of 1890 varied from 12 to 24 cents per pound and 35 per cent ad valorem, and that the duties at the present time are 49½ cents per pound and 60

727.

per cent ad valorem, equivalent to an ad valorem rate of from 140 to 186 per cent.

The goods in question, unless made up into garments as is certainly not contemplated by the description, would be dutiable under paragraph 392 of the act of 1890, at 44 cents a pound and 50 per cent ad valorem, instead of at 49½ cents per pound and 60 per cent ad valorem.

If classified as manufactures of worsted, they would have paid a duty prior to the passage of the act of 1890 of 35 cents per pound and 35 per cent ad valorem, instead of from 12 to 24 cents per pound, as stated by Mr. McKeever.

It is singular that Mr. McKeever should have taken as a basis for his comparison of the rates imposed on astrachans, in one case the lowest rate levied by the wool schedule of the act of 1883, that upon flannels and blankets, and in the other case the highest rate imposed upon manufactures of wool by the act of 1890, that upon ready-made clothing, when neither of the rates was applicable to the goods in question.

Mr. McKeever is a man of keen intelligence, wonderfully familiar with tariff rates and the effect of tariff changes upon his business as an importer, and it is difficult to understand how he could have subscribed to a statement so strangely inaccurate.

Samples Nos. 10 to 17, inclusive, are at present dutiable, under paragraph 394, as women's and children's dress goods, coat linings, etc. By the provisions of the act of 1890 the dividing line of value in this class of goods, upon which higher duties were levied, was reduced from 20 to 15 cents per yard. This change was made to meet the great decline that had taken place in the price of goods of this character between 1883 and 1890. It will be noticed that Mr. McKeever has taken in all instances for his comparison of rates goods that are included within this changed limit. In no other manner could such disparity in rates be shown.

There is another feature of this statement in regard to the change in the rates on dress goods which requires attention. By a construction of the act of 1883, which was clearly erroneous, certain goods weighing over 4 ounces per square yard were admitted upon the payment of the square-yard duty, instead of the pound-duty, which it was the purpose of the act of 1883 to impose. This manifest defect in the law was remedied by the provisions of the act of 1890. and the effect of this remedial legislation is represented in the table as an increase in rates. It is true the duties were advanced, as stated in the table, on samples Nos. 1 to 9, inclusive. The purpose of these advanced rates was clearly stated at the time the bill was passed. Neither cotton velvets, corduroys, nor silk-striped sleeve linings had been made to any considerable extent in the United States prior to the passage of the act, and it was the intention of the framers of the bill to give to these articles adequate protection, in order that the American producer could have an equal chance to secure the American market. Their success in this direction has been especiall/ gratifying.

This disposes, I believe, of the question of relative rates, and I will now take up the question, Does the table show an increase in prices or cost of necessaries of life, as claimed by the Senator from Missouri?

The articles named are not in any sense necessaries of life, and it will be extremely difficult for the Senator from Missouri to make the plain people of the country believe that silk-striped sleeve linings, astrachans, cotton velvets, and corduroys belong to that class. They certainly do not, and none of the articles in McKeever's list, with the possible exception of coat linings, go into use to any considerable extent in the households of the poor.

But whatever their character, the most important fact to be inquired into in connection with this table, and the purposes for which it is exhibited, is whether the provisions of the act of 1890 had the effect to advance the cost to consumers of these articles or others similar in character or used for similar purposes.

As I have already said, Mr. McKeever's statement contains no evidence that the prices of the articles named have advanced, but that the cost to import them is slightly greater since the passage of the act of 1890. The fact is disclosed, however, that the increased cost as stated does not in any case equal the additional duty. The consumers of the country, however, for whom the distinguished Senator from Missouri assumes sometimes to speak, are not especially interested in the slight increase of cost to import the goods in question, or in the percentage of profit which Mr. McKeever and his associates realize from their importations. The question to be determined in their behalf is whether the prices that they pay for these or similar goods have been advanced.

I shall endeavor to satisfy Senators that every purchaser of these goods or similar goods for consumption, whether of domestic or foreign manufacture, can buy them to-day at lower prices than those current prior to 1890.

While the articles named by Mr. McKeever as " women's and children's dress goods " are exceptional in their character and comparatively unimportant, it is true that the general class of goods included in the designation is very important, and we may well address ourselves to an investigation of the fact whether the articles included in this class, in common use, have increased in price. I submit herewith a statement showing the prices at which goods of domestic manufacture, the general class of dress goods which enter most largely into consumption, sold in the month of July in the years 1890, 1891, and 1892:

Prices of coat linings and woman's and children's dress goods.

	Width.	July, 1890.	July, 1891.	July, 1892.
COAT LININGS AND ITALIAN CLOTH.				
Farr Alpaca Company. Holyoke, Mass.:	*Inches.*	*Cents.*	*Cents.*	*Cents.*
Double-warp coat linings	32	28	28	27¾
Single-warp coat linings	32	27	27	26¼
DRESS GOODS.				
Manchester Mills, Manchester, N. H.:				
"813" cashmere	35	19	18½	18
Arlington Mills. Lawrence, Mass.:				
Cotton warp cashmere, No. 100	34 to 35	18½	18½	18
Cotton warp cashmere, No. 200	35 to 36	22	22	21¼
Atlantic Mills, Providence, R. I.:				
Atlantic's Fs	35	19	18	18
Atlantic's FFs	35	25	23¾	23¾
Hamilton Woolen Company, Southbridge, Mass.:				
Cashmere	27	10	10	9¾

It will be noticed that the Farr Alpaca Company, of Holyoke, Mass., quote double and single warp coat linings at a lower rate in July, 1892, than in either of the previous years. The other quotations submitted by me are the prices at which the goods manufactured by the five leading American producers of women's and children's dress goods sold their product at the respective dates named. These quotations show a decline in price in every case.

These quotations refer only to domestic goods; but a very large proportion of the goods of this class consumed in the United States is produced by the domestic manufacturers, who have practically the control of the American market.

It can, however, be conclusively established that the cost to import the great mass of women's and children's dress goods is less to-day than it was before the passage of the act of 1890, and it is certainly true that both foreign and domestic goods of this character are sold at retail at lower prices now than they were prior to October, 1890. I have been furnished by Messrs. William H. Burgess & Co., of Paris and New York, with a statement showing the foreign cost and the cost to lay down in New York, duty paid, of all-wool cashmeres, standard quality, 12 to 13 twill. Other descriptions of all-wool dress goods vary in price with these at a fixed ratio. This statement shows that the cost to import the goods in question, duty and other charges paid, in 1887, was 44.2 cents; in 1888, 42.8 cents; in 1889, 41.4 cents, and in 1892, 40 cents per yard. This would seem to clearly establish the fact that for the great mass of women's and children's dress goods used in the United States the cost laid down in New York to the importer is less prior to-day to than was it tariff changes.

In regard to the price of astrachans there is very little to be said. The demand for this fabric is extremely limited, and fluctuations in the price are of very little importance to the people of the country. I have, however, been furnished with samples and a price list of astrachans of domestic manufacture by the Goodall Worsted Company, of Sanford, Me. This list shows that the company referred to sells 54-inch astrachans, 50 ounces in weight, at $3.63 per yard net to their customers, or at 97 cents per yard less than the cost of importing similar goods, as reported by Mr. McKeever.

I submit a table showing the comparative prices at which silk sleeve linings were sold for consumption prior to October, 1890, and in 1892:

727

Prices of silk striped sleeve linings.

Quality.	Width.	Price in 1889.	Price in 1890 after bill was passed.	Price in 1892.	Difference in price, lower.
	Inches.	*Cents.*	*Cents.*	*Cents.*	*Cents.*
No. 1	40	87.5	36	34.7	2.8
No. 2	40	56	40.5	38.30	17.7
No. 3	40	60	49.5	47.25	12.75
No. 4	40	62.5	54	51.8	10.7
No. 5	40	73	60 .	58.5	14.5

This table shows a decline in prices in all cases varying from 2.8 cents per yard to 17.7 cents per yard. I will also have printed in the RECORD a letter from the Royal Weaving Company, of Pawtucket, R. I., explaining this statement.

I have in my possession samples of all the goods on which prices are quoted in the various tables I have submitted.

It is undoubtedly true that the price of most descriptions of cotton velvet and corduroys included in Mr. McKeever's table are somewhat higher to-day than they were in 1889 and 1890, just prior to the passage of the McKinley act. An effort was made in the years 1887, 1888, and 1889 to establish the industry of the manufacture of cotton velvets in this country; but in 1889 and 1890 the prices were reduced so low by the foreign manufacturers as to drive most of the American producers out of the market; and while it is true that there has been a reaction in prices, it is also true that prices in 1892 on all classes of goods are less than they were in 1885. The rapid decline which took place in 1889 and 1890 is shown by the fact that goods which sold in 1885 for 29¼ cents, sold in 1889 for 17½ cents, and the price of similar goods in 1892 was 23½ cents. Another quality which sold in 1885 for 36 cents, sold in 1890 at 27 cents. and the present price is 28 cents. The slight increase which has taken place since 1890 has by no means restored prices to the level of the years 1885–1887.

In what I have said in regard to the increased cost of cotton velvets and corduroys this year as compared with 1890, I have only had reference to the prices at which the goods were sold either by importers or manufacturers. The retail prices of these goods to consumers are in most cases lower now than prior to the passage of the act of 1890.

The great disparity between the retail price and wholesale price of cotton velvets was shown by me in the course of the discussion of the tariff bill of 1890. It was then claimed by the importers that certain cotton velvets were sold abroad at 12 cents a yard. The lowest price at which any cotton velvet could then be purchased at any dry-goods store in Washington at re-tail was 60 cents per yard. It is very evident that the slight reduction in the importers' profits which has been recently ef-fected would have no perceptible influence upon the retail price.

I think I have effectually disposed of Mr. McKeever's state-ments as the basis of a claim that prices have been advanced by the tariff legislation of the Fifty-first Congress.

The table which I have had under examination contained the only evidence furnished by the Senator from Missouri in support of his claim, except a statement made in regard to the price of hard-ware. Giving a New York evening paper as authority, he stated that the price of hardware had advanced from 30 to 57½ per cent. It is apparent, however, that instead of hardware the Senator from Missouri intended to say cutlery, as certainly the prices of gen-eral hardware, are very much lower to-day than prior to 1890. Bearing upon the question as to whether an increase has taken place in the price of table cutlery, I will state, upon the author-ity of Charles S. Landers, of Landers, Frary & Clarke, of New Britain, Conn., large table-cutlery manufacturers, that the prices on the entire line of goods manufactured by them are at least 7½ per cent lower now than they were in October, 1890, and that no advance has taken place since that time. I will print Mr. Lan-der's letter in the RECORD.

In regard to the price of pocket cutlery, I have received a let-ter from Mr. W. F. Rockwell, of Miller Brothers' Cutlery Com-pany, which contains the following statement:

As to prices on American pocket cutlery. Many patterns have not been advanced at all. Several styles that have been sold below actual cost have been advanced so they now pay a small profit.

The average advances do not exceed 10 per cent to the jobbing trade. The margin of profit between the jobber and consumer was sufficient, so there was no reason or necessity of advancing the price to the consumer, and it has not been done.

The wages of pocket-cutlery workers have been advanced from 5 per cent to 25 per cent in the different operations. One of the oldest foremen in the country estimates that the advances which have been made in wages, together with the more steady work given the men, will furnish them at least an average of 20 per cent more annual income.

Many of the factories have more than doubled their capacity in buildings and machinery, and all of them show increased production. The gain in output, of course, reduces incidental expenses.

The fact that the value of the pocket cutlery imported last year, with the duty added. so closely approximates the amount made here, shows the conditions of competition pretty accurately adjusted.

I have taken pains to make a very full and complete analysis, which I fear the Senate has found technical and tedious in its character, of the statements made by the Senator from Missouri for the purpose of showing how completely they fail in every respect to establish the claim that articles in general use have been advanced in price as a result of the tariff legislation of two years ago.

After having attempted to show that the rates imposed by the acts of 1890 had increased the cost of necessaries of life, the Senator from Missouri attempts to establish the fact that these rates were not necessary for the protection of the labor employed in the different industries in this country. He even goes so far as to say that labor at the present time is cheaper in the United States than anywhere else in the world. To use his own language:

It is well known to those who make these statements that the American operatives, from their superior energy and intelligence, can successfully compete with any labor in the world, and that American labor is the cheapest in the world, because it produces a better article.

To confirm this assertion the Senator quotes from statements made by Mr. J. Shoenhof, which purport to show that the cost of labor in the production of leading articles manfactured in the United States is but little if any more in any case, and in many cases less than in competing countries in Europe. Statements of this nature are frequently made for the purpose of showing that tariff rates are excessive. Their inaccuracy has been frequently exposed. All must admit that there are no statistics in existence that can be possibly made to show that the earnings of labor in any occupation or profession are not much greater in the United States than in any of the countries with whom we compete in the production of manufactured articles.

The recent investigation of the Finance Committee showed that in certain general occupations wages in the United States were 77 per cent higher than in England. I have submitted tables

727

showing the relative wages in cotton and worsted mills in the two countries, with American wages in many cases more than 100 per cent higher. The tables in reference to wages in the production of tin plate, which I submit, show a difference of 152 per cent in favor of the United States as compared with Wales. Similar statistics are abundant. Wages in the United States show a still greater excess when compared with those of the countries of Continental Europe. This difference is undoubtedly greater in certain occupations and localities than in others.

There is no evidence, moreover, to show that Mr. Shoenhof's figures relate to the labor cost of production of the same descriptions of goods in the United States and in England. For instance, in the statement in regard to weaving and finishing 6–4 worsted cloths, there is nothing to indicate the character of the goods except the width.

These and similar statements of Mr. Shoenhof's have been frequently published, and practical manufacturers, familiar with the conditions on both sides of the ocean, have repeatedly demonstrated in this Chamber and elsewhere that they are not only worthless, but sometimes grotesque in their excess of misinformation.

Tariff reformers, as a rule, admit that American earnings are greater than any others, but assume that the higher rates of wages here insure lower cost of production on account of the greater skill and efficiency of American workmen. This, they assert, is the necessary result of the general economic law that high wages produce low cost of production.

There are many instances in which the producers of the United States, through the superior energy, skill, and genius of our mechanics and inventors, or by the greater or more effective use of machinery, have reduced the cost of production to a point lower than that in competing countries. In these cases import duties are of course inoperative. The number of cases in which this is true is constantly increasing. If the act of 1890 is allowed to remain upon the statute books until the full benefit of its provisions can be realized the list of articles in which we can successfully compete is certain to be greatly enlarged.

Notwithstanding the superior activity and intelligence of

727——2

American workmen and all the other industrial advantages
which we have, it is undoubtedly as true to-day as it was in 1888
that the cost to the American manufacturer of accomplishing
certain equivalent results, that is of producing say a yard of cotton or woolen cloth, or a ton of iron or steel of the same or similar quality, is in most instances much greater than to his foreign
competitor, owing to the much greater cost here of labor and
services in production, and in all collateral employments. The
actual relative conditions which govern production are with the
exceptions I have noted, these: The American manufacturer and
his foreign competitor both use the same machinery, which runs
at the same speed, an equal number of hours, turning out the
same quantity and kind of goods. Under these circumstances it
is evident that the higher wages paid in the United States result in a greater cost of production, and it is to maintain this
higher level of wages and at the same time to equalize conditions of production that protective duties are levied.

It is of course impossible to determine the exact rate of duty
to be levied upon any article by a comparison of the single element of wages, or even the relative earnings of labor in different countries. This proposition seems too plain to need discussion. It is equally impossible to adjust tariff rates levied to equalize conditions, on the basis of the mathematical relation which the
labor cost at one stage bears to the finished product, as, for instance, the proportion which the cost of weaving bears to the
completed fabric.

The rule that should apply in fixing the rates of protective
duties is that they should in all cases equal the difference between the cost of production and distribution, under normal conditions, of the article in question in our own and in that competing country where the cost of production is lowest. This was the
rule which was followed in the preparation of the act of 1890, and
of the Senate tariff bill of 1888, which formed the basis of this
measure.

Protective duties levied in this manner have but one purpose
and can have but one effect, that is, to protect American labor
and to maintain the existing high level of wages and earnings of
American workmen. When such duties are removed or reduced

below the protective point labor receives the full force of the blow.

While it is not claimed that protective tariffs guarantee any particular scale of wages in any particular industry and while tariff rates can not be based directly on the difference in ascertained wages, or even in the relative earnings of people in competing countries, it will be readily seen that, by the rule I have laid down, this difference becomes really the basis upon which all duties are levied, as tariff rates are fixed by the difference in the cost of production between competing countries, and the difference in the cost of production in the final analysis, consists of a difference in wages or earnings.

This rule for fixing rates should only apply, however, to articles in the production of which the United States has equal natural advantages with other countries. As a protectionist I believe that the United States can not afford, having in view the most rapid development of her great resources, to levy duties upon articles in the production of which other countries have permanent natural advantages. Such articles should be admitted free. In the case of articles fairly entitled to protection, the rule that I have laid down, I believe, is the only one that should be followed.

Tariff rates are frequently criticised because certain statistical reports show that the so-called percentage of labor cost of production in a particular article is less than the rate of duty imposed upon that article, and it is assumed therefore that the rates are unnecessarily high. For instance, these reports purport to show that the percentage of labor cost in producing woolen goods is from 22 to 25 per cent of the total cost of the product, and therefore it is argued that the rate of duty should not exceed that rate. Statistics of this nature, taking into consideration only the labor employed in a single stage in the long process of manufacture as a basis for the ratio, may have some value statistically, but they have no value whatever in determining the rate of duties which should be imposed by a protective tariff. For instance, knowledge of the exact percentage of cost in each case which the cost of riveting a blade into a pocket knife bears to the total cost of the knife in Meriden, in Sheffield, or in Solingen, would be of no special value to a legislator. Protective duties are levied to equalize conditions, ana it is the total relative cost of producing the completed knife at these competing points and not the relation which the cost of riveting or polishing the blade has to this that should determine equalizing rates.

All refinements of calculation in regard to percentages of labor cost are therefore entirely useless in a discussion of the tariff rates. If it costs $1 to produce a yard of woolen cloth in Massachusetts. and 60 cents in France, the natural advantages of the United States being equal to France in the production of woolen cloth, it would be necessary in order to equalize conditions to levy a duty of 40 cents a yard. It is comparatively easy for a legislator to ascertain differences in the total cost of production, but quite impossible for him to determine the mathematical relation of partial costs at different stages.

From this point of view much valuable time has also been wasted in the collection and discussion of statistics in regard to so-called total labor cost of production. Most of these statistics leave out of the computation sums paid for clerical service, for superintendence, for taxes and insurance, for labor in repairs and materials, and all the great mass of incidental expenses which go to make up the cost of doing business, and the ultimate cost of production. These all represent labor or services. The sums collected for taxes, for instance, go to pay school-teachers, firemen, policemen, tax assessors, collectors, and various other employés in the public service. All the essential elements in the cost of production can be reduced to an expenditure for labor or services in some form, and labor cost of production and total cost of product are equal terms.

Among the many remarkable statements made by the Senator from Missouri in his speech of June 28, I find the following:

I am prepared to show by irrefutable testimony that never in the history of this country has there been such disturbance of labor. never such hostile and inimical relations between employer and employé, never such prostration of agricultural interests, never such a limiting and narrowing of foreign markets, never such disaster brought about in so short a time as by this infamous legislation.

It will be noticed that this sentence contains three distinct charges in regard to the operations of the act of 1890, and these

727

I propose to take up seriatim. The first of these is that there had never been such disturbance in labor, never such hostile relations between employer and employé, as were brought about by the act referred to. In support of this allegation the Senator submitted and had printed in the RECORD a long list of alleged "wage reductions, shut-downs, lock-outs, and strikes in protected manufactures which had taken place sinbe the passage of the McKinley bill from data collected by Hon. JOHN DE WITT WARNER for the New York World." This list covers the time between December 4, 1890, and June 18, 1892, a period of eighteen months.

The statement shows that during this period seventy-seven strikes occurred in the United States. If we assume that these figures are accurate, and it will be seen from an examination of the other papers furnished by the same gentleman that he has a decided tendency to overstate in his statistics, it may be profitable to make a comparison between the number of strikes occurring as alleged since the passage of the act of 1890 and in the years which preceded it.

Having this comparison in mind, I requested the Commissioner of Labor to furnish me with statistics of strikes in this country for the years prior to 1890, and if possible to give me comparative statistics of strikes which have taken place in Great Britain within the period covered by his American statistics.

In answer to this request I have received the following table, showing the number of strikes and the number of employés involved in each year, from 1880 to 1890, inclusive, in the United States:

Years.	Number of strikes.	Employés striking and involved.
1880	610	
1881	471	129,521
1882	454	154,671
1883	478	149,763
1884	443	147.054
1885	645	242,705
1886	1,411	499,489
1887	872	345,073
1888	679	211,016
1889	643	177,298
1890	798	201,682

It will be noticed that the number of strikes in this country varied from 443 in 1884 to 1,411 in 1886; the average number of each year for the whole period being 625. The number reported in 1890 is 798, being more than ten times as many in this single year as reported by Mr. WARNER for the eighteen months covered by his statistics.

Available statistics show that in Great Britain, the paradise of tariff reformers, 3,164 strikes occurred in 1889. The British Board of Trade officially report 1,028 strikes in 1890, with 392,-981 persons involved in 738 of these.

It will be seen by a comparison of the relative number and importance of strikes in the United States and in Great Britain for the year 1890 that the number was much greater in the latter country, and that the number of persons involved was more than three times as great in proportion to the number of persons engaged in useful occupations in the respective countries.

In the recent strike in the Durham (English) district 100,000 coal miners went out and remained idle from March 12 to June 1, when they accepted a reduction of 10 per cent in wages. This strike involved the closing down of one hundred blast furnaces in addition to the suspension of mining operations.

The statistics submitted by the Senator from Missouri confirm in a striking manner the judgment of every intelligent observer, that there has been a remarkable freedom from strikes and labor troubles in this country since the passage of the tariff act of 1890. It can be said that at no time in the history of the country has labor been so constantly and profitably employed, and at such satisfactory wages as in the period referred to. No person in the United States with the capacity and willingness to work is out of employment.

It is true that a reduction of wages has taken place in a limited number of establishments producing iron and steel; but the fact should not be overlooked that even with this reduction, the average wages are still much higher than in any of the other great industries. The earnings in some departments are exceptionally high; for instance, the average net earnings of bar rollers in all the Pittsburg mills is $15.25 per day, and the net earnings in wire rod rolling are even higher than this.

Mr. WARNER'S table contains several items in regard to reductions in wages said to have been made in the Rhode Island
and Fall River cotton mills, in November, 1890, and in 1891. I
can say on the authority of the representatives of the mills in
question that these statements are entirely untrue, and that no
such reductions took place.

From such examination as I have been able to make, I can say
that the various statements in regard to reductions of wages in
cotton mills are equally untrue.

Many of the items contained in Mr. WARNER'S list of reductions are of the most absurd character. For instance, we find
the following under date of September 24, 1891:

Reduction of wages in the entire cotton industry is feared by the workmen
at Providence, Pawtucket, and other cities in Rhode Island, but they will re-
sort to a general strike rather than submit to a reduction in their miserable
pittance, which is already bordering on the starvation level.

There was not the slightest foundation for this sensational report. On the contrary, at the time named considerable cotton
machinery was idle in Rhode Island from the fact that the sup-
ply of help was not equal to the demand.

Mr. WARNER'S list is largely made up of similar inconsequen-
tial and absurd statements.

It is perhaps proper that I should say a word in regard to the
condition and earnings of the operatives in Rhode Island.

That they do not work for a miserable pittance is shown by a
statement which I submit and will have printed in the RECORD,
of the relative wages paid in a cotton mill in Rhode Island and
one in Oldham, England, showing the much greater wages in
Rhods Island. The mills have each about 63,000 spindles and
make the same kind of goods. This table was furnished me by
my friend, lately an honored member of the Senate, Hon. Jon-
athan Chace.

Instead of working at "starvation wages" the working people
of my State are enabled from their earnings to live as well and as
comfortably as any similar class of people in the world; and their
savings, averaging nearly $1,000 for each family, deposited in
the saving banks of the State, furnish the best evidence of their
prosperous and satisfactory condition. These savings, accumu-
lated since the inauguration of the protective policy of the United

727

States, are greater per capita. I believe. than those of any other industrial community in the world.

Many of the items in the list of strikes and reductions are inserted several times, apparently in order to swell the number.

The following letter from S. N. D. North, secretary of the National Association of Wool Manufacturers, answers the statements contained in that portion of the table submitted by the Senator from Missouri which relates to reduction in wages, strikes, etc., in woolen mills:

NATIONAL ASSOCIATION OF WOOL MANUFACTURERS,
Boston, Mass., July 20, 1892.

DEAR SIR: Such inquiries as I have been able to make justify my previous statement that there have been no reductions of wages in the wool manufacture since the passage of the McKinley law: on the contrary, there have been many increases, and there was never a time when so many operatives were so steadily employed in this industry as at present.

The Warner list of alleged "strikes and reductions," so far as relates to woolens and worsteds, is a mass of falsehoods, duplications, errors, and misstatements. Of the twenty-five entries that appear under this head, five are duplications of each other: eight are about cotton mills, and one relates to a silk mill. So far as items 6, 17, and 21 are concerned, I refer you to the inclosed letter of the Titus Sheard Company, of Little Falls, N. Y., which shows them all to be false, the facts being directly the reverse of those stated.

Items 9 and 20, stating reductions and strikes at the Arlington Mills, are both false. There have been readjustments of the method of payment in this mill, under which both the weavers and the wool-sorters earn as much, if not more, than before these readjustments were made; and, as a matter of fact, the Arlington Mills' operatives are now receiving sixty hours pay for fifty-eight hours' work, which involves an increase of 3½ per cent.

No. 22, regarding the Atlantic Mills, is wholly false. There has been no change of wages or trouble of any kind in that mill since it passed under the present management.

The only item in the whole twenty-five for which I can find any basis in truth is the Wanskuck Mills, who did attempt a reduction in weavers' wages, which led to a strike of 350 weavers. The complaint in the Weybosset was adjusted by placing the weavers on the same tariff that prevailed in the neighboring mills.

No. 23.—There has been no strike or reduction in the mills of Switz Condé at Oswego.

The only cases remaining are No. 2, in Illinois, and No. 24, in Delaware, about which I know nothing. If investigated, I have no doubt the facts would show that there have been no reductions in these cases. Mr. WARNER has made up a formidable-looking list by seizing upon every item of newspaper gossip and failing to ascertain in any instance the real facts or the actual outcome. To one familiar with the facts it seems as though Mr. WARNER ought to be heartily ashamed of himself.

I have now answered, to the best of my ability, every question you have addressed to me.

Very respectfully,

S. N. D. NORTH, *Secretary.*

Hon. NELSON W. ALDRICH,
United States Senate.

727

[Inclosure.]

TITUS SHEARD COMPANY, EAGLE MILLS,
Little Falls, N. Y., July 14, 1892.

DEAR SIR: In reply to yours of the 13th would say that the claim made that we reduced wages in 1891 or since is entirely false; in fact, we have increased the wages of a number of our operatives since the above date. This is about the same condition in the other mills mentioned in your correspondence. We think it can be safely said that never in the history of the knitting industry have the employés been making as good wages as at the present time and for the past year; also, that the mills are well employed; in fact, a number running over time, some all night with two sets of hands. Some time during 1891 we went on a new class of work, and in adjusting the wages we were obliged to do it entirely by guess. After running a few months we found that we were paying too much, and the girls which were on this class of work were able to earn from $5 to $6 a day. We made a slight reduction on this work alone, and they are now able to make from $2 to $3 a day when steadily on this class of work.

We shall be pleased to furnish you with any further information in our power.

Yours, very truly,

TITUS SHEARD COMPANY.

Mr. S. N. D. NORTH, *Boston, Mass.*

I believe that I have conclusively shown the worthless character of the evidence submitted by the Senator from Missouri to substantiate his claim that the relations between employer and employé are of a hostile and unsatisfactory character.

That there is constant movement towards a higher level of wages in this country is shown by the reports of the Eleventh Census on the textile industries of the United States. These reports show a considerable increase in wages in every branch. The investigation by the Senate Finance Committee into wages from June, 1889, to September, 1891, showed an average increase for the occupations included in the inquiry of three-fourths of 1 per cent. All similar examinations reveal the existence of a tendency to higher rates.

Contentions between employers and employés over rates of wages, hours of employment, etc., occur in times of prosperity and in periods of business depression. No country in the world is free from them, and their recurrence does not usually indicate hostile relations. They are not the outgrowth of any revenue system, but their number and importance has been, as I have shown, reduced to a minimum under recent protective legislation. The process of evolution is often a process of disturbance, and through disputes over rates of wages, usually of friendly character, just conclusions are reached.

727

The next statement by the Senator from Missouri to which I shall call attention is that there has never been such prostration of agricultural interests as was effected by the act of 1890. In support of this statement no evidence whatever was submitted. No assertion could be more diametrically opposed to the actual facts of the case than this.

In no class of people in the United States has the improvement in condition been so marked as in the farmers during the period under consideration.

The relative condition of the agricultural interests, as shown by the inquiry of the Finance Committee, to which I have already alluded, is briefly this:

The prices received for farm products subsequent to the passage of the act of 1890 shows an average increase on all crops of 18.67 per cent. The percentage of increase on many important articles—corn, for instance, at 47 per cent—was greatly above this average.

It will be seen by an examination of the report of the committee that the advance in the average price of all cereals, the computation being made according to their relative importance, was 33.59 per cent. The price received for meats of all kind averaged 4 per cent higher in September, 1891, than in June, 1889.

The most striking result shown by the inquiry was the fact that while there was a considerable decline in the prices of manufactured acticles which enter into general consumption there was an advance in the price of nearly all agricultural products; and if it had not been for the great decline that took place in the price of sugar, owing to removal of duties by the act of 1890, that large portion of the cost of living which is embraced in expenditures for food would have shown an increase instead of diminution.

During the period covered by the investigation of the Finance Committee there were several months in which the prices were higher than for the initial period of the investigation. In each of these cases the increased average grew solely out of the advances in price of agricultural products. This is illustrated by the list which follows, of the articles which were advanced in

727

price in April, 1891, to such an extent as to increase the average for that month to a point considerably above the general average:

Milk, fresh; turkey, dressed; cheese, mutton, beef, roasting; oysters, prunes, California; peaches, canned; oleomargarine, meal, corn, butter, best creamery; eggs, apples, dried; turnips, butter, dairy; onions, cabbages, potatoes, tomatoes, fresh.

The prices of the articles which it is necessary for the farmer to buy for the support of his family and for carrying on the operations of his farm, were reduced in the period subsequent to the passage of the act on an average 2 per cent below the prices current prior to that time.

The percentage of reduction which took place in the prices of the class of articles the farmer has to purchase is shown by the following table taken from the report of the committee, the price prior to passage of the act being represented by 100:

Group.	Retail.
Cloths and clothing	99. 65
Fuel and lighting	98. 69
Metals and implements	97. 49
Lumber and building material	98. 28
Drugs and chemicals	95. 96
House-furnishing goods	93. 82
Miscellaneous	100. 52

It is not necessary for the purposes of my argument to assume that the advance in farm prices of agricultural products was due entirely to the operations of the act of 1890. I am treating at this time the statement of the Senator from Missouri as to the actual facts. I believe that in no period of equal length in the history of the country has there been such a marked improvement in the condition of any class of people as can be shown, using the language of the Senator from Missouri, by irrefutable testimony, to have taken place in the condition of the farmers of this country since the passage of the act of 1890.

There has been a great advance in the sum received by them for their crops and a substantial decline in prices of articles, especially manufactured products, which they are obliged to purchase. The farmer to-day, with an equal number of bushels of

727

grain or pounds of meat, can buy more and better clothing, machinery, or supplies, than ever before. Within this period hundreds of millions of dollars of their indebtedness have been paid off, and as a class their financial condition vastly improved. By the operations of the act of 1890 the farmers were given larger and more profitable markets both at home and abroad; as an instance of this our exports to Cuba—largely of agricultural products—were increased during the ten months ending June 30, 1892, as compared with the corresponding ten months of the previous fiscal year, $5,700,000, or an increase of 54.86 per cent.

It is quite natural for all classes of people to believe that their condition ought to be and might be improved, but the assurance displayed in this Chamber in the attempts to convince the farmer, in the face of the facts which I have recited, that he is suffering untold evils as the result of tariff legislation, has no parallel.

The next statement made by the Senator from Missouri, to which I will call attention, is "That there had never been such a limiting and narrowing of foreign markets" as since the passage of the act of 1890. This statement is equally astounding with the others I have alluded to, and equally at variance with the facts.

The foreign commerce of the United States for the fiscal year ending June 30. 1892, consisted of imports of the value of $827,391,284, and of exports of the value of $1,030,335,626, or a total value of imports and exports of $1,857,726,910.

The following shows the rapid growth of our foreign commerce:

Foreign commerce of the United States.

IMPORTS AND EXPORTS.

Years.	Annual average.	Per capita.
Total imports and exports:		
1847 to 1861	$553,000,000	$17.08
1876 to 1890	1,356,000,000	25.20
1892	1,857,724,910	28.32
Imports:		
1847 to 1861	348,000,000	9.35
1876 to 1890	626,000,000	11.63
1892	827,391,284	12.61
Exports:		
1847 to 1861	205,000,000	7.73
1876 to 1890	730,000,000	13.57
1892	1,030,335,626	15.71

This table contains a comparison of the annual values of total commerce and of imports and exports, and the amount of each per capita for the fifteen years of the revenue-tariff period, 1847-1861, and the fifteen years which preceded the adoption of the act of 1890, and for the first fiscal year after all the provisions of this act went into effect. No other country can show such a record of expansion and development.

I submit a table showing the total imports and exports of merchandise and the excess of exports over imports for the fiscal years 1884 to 1892, inclusive.

It will be seen that the excess of exports over imports, or balance of trade in our favor was $202,944,342, in 1892 an excess of exports over imports that has been exceeded in amount but three times in the history of the country.

I also submit a table showing the proportion of dutiable to free imports, and the average ad valorem rate collected on dutiable imports and on all imports for the years 1889 to 1892, inclusive.

It will be observed that the ad valorem rate on all importations for the fiscal year 1892 was 20.65 per cent, the lowest rate since 1861, and a lower rate than the average imposed by the act of 1846.

The following table shows the percentage of free and dutiable importations under each of our tariff laws enacted since 1847:

Importations under the various tariff laws, from 1847 to 1892. Percentages of free and dutiable.

Period.	Dutiable.	Free.
	Per ct.	Per ct.
1847 to 1857	88	12
1858 to 1861	78	22
1879 to 1883	70	30
1884 to 1890	66.5	33.5
1892	44.6	55.4

This table discloses the rapid growth of the free list with advances in protective legislation. The tables taken together furnish convincing evidence to disprove the statement so freely made as to the restrictive effects of such legislation on foreign commerce.

727

An analysis of details of both imports and exports will develop the fact that desirable changes have taken place in the character of each. The exports of manufactured and other articles exclusive of all farm and agricultural products and petroleum, amounted in value in 1892 to $237,665,370. This value of exportation of manufactured articles, etc., it will be observed, is $32,-000,000 greater than the total average annual value of all exports for the period 1847 to 1861.

I also present a table, which I will have printed, showing the value of the exports of the leading products for each year from 1888 to 1892, inclusive. The amount of duty per capita collected during the fiscal year 1892 was $2.62; that is, less than half the relative amount collected in 1872, the amount for the latter year having been $5.28 per capita.

These statements and comparisons must be extremely gratifying to every patriotic American. They show beyond any possibility of doubt that the expansion of our foreign commerce was accelerated rather than narrowed and limited by the act of 1890, as stated by the Senator from Missouri.

A considerable portion of the speech delivered by the Senator from Missouri on the 6th of June was devoted to a consideration of the duties on wool and woolens, in which the Senator endeavored to prove that these duties have been injurious alike to wool-growers, woolen manufacturers, and consumers.

In discussing the effect which the tariff on wool has upon the American wool-grower, the Senator from Missouri said:

The wool-grower in this country has not received one cent of this protection; and I shall prove by figures that every dollar of it has gone into the pockets of the manufacturers and will continue to go there. * * * No man can show that these enormous tariffs benefited the wool-growers of the United States. It was impossible that they could have done so, because the wool-growers received no part of the bounty. * * * For twenty-three years the wool-grower of the United States had never received more than one-fourth of a cent a pound higher price for his wool than the wool-grower of England.

In reply to a question by the Senator from Mississippi [Mr. GEORGE] in regard to this latter statement, the Senator from Missouri said that these prices " were for the same quality of wool."

727

This assertion that the prices of wool of equal quality are and have been for many years substantially the same in the United States and in Great Britain is made the basis of most of the arguments that have recently been made in favor of the removal of the duties on wool.

In support of the assertion, the Senator from Missouri relies, first, upon a comparison of certain reports of the Treasury Department, giving the average foreign price of all wools imported, with the reports of the Department of Agriculture, giving the farm prices of the wool produced in the United States; and second, a statement prepared by Mr. S. N. D. North, the secretary of the National Wool Manufacturers' Association, giving the relative prices for a series of years of medium Ohio fleece in the United States, and Port Phillip fleece in London.

The reports of the Treasury Department and the Department of Agriculture, referred to by the Senator, afford no basis whatever for a comparison between the prices of foreign and domestic wool of the same or similar grades or qualities, as they are the average of prices for all kinds, and just what kinds are included in the average in any case is not known. It is true, however, that the statement furnished by Mr. North does apply to specific grades of wool and to grades that for many years have sold in London and the United States at substantially the same prices. They are, however, sold in their respective markets in very different conditions, and the net cost of cleaned wool to purchasers is widely different. The Senator from Missouri was not aware, I am sure, that Mr. North had protested in a published letter against the use which had been made of his figures. Mr. North's calculations of the relative shrinkage of the two grades of wool establishes the fact that the difference in their actual value was about equal to the wool duties levied by our tariff. The Australian wools are sold skirted, while the Ohio wools are not.

For the purpose of showing the actual cost to an American manufacturer of a pound of scoured domestic wool purchased in the United States as compared with the cost to his English competitor of a pound of scoured wool of similar quality in

727

London, I submit the following table, which shows the average annual price for each of the twelve years, 1881 to 1892, inclusive, of a scoured pound of fine Ohio fleece in the United States, and of average Australian fleece in London:

Comparison of prices of Ohio and Australian wools.

Year.	Price of fine Ohio fleece, scoured.	Price in London of Australian average fleece, scoured.	Difference of the two prices.
1881	$0.95½	$0.53	$0.42½
1882	.90½	.53	.37½
1883	.86	.51	.35
1884	.80½	.48	.32½
1885	.71¼	.41	.30¼
1886	.74	.41	.33
1887	.73¼	.42	.31¼
1888	.68	.42	.26
1889	.73½	.48	.25½
1890	.73¼	.44	.29¼
1891	.70¾	.40	.30¾
1892	.62¼	.32	.30¼

Average difference for the twelve years, 32 cents.

The prices for Ohio fleece are furnished by Messrs. Mauger & Avery, of Boston, Mass., and the London prices are furnished by Helmuth, Schwartze & Co., the well-known London wool-brokers.

It will be seen by these figures which are furnished by those highest in authority in their respective countries, that the American farmer or wool-grower received the full benefit of the tariff on wool, and that he obtains on an average 32 cents more per pound for his wool, not including dirt and other impurities, than his Australian competitor. The price of the pound of clean wool is of course the only test of actual relative value to the manufacturer, as this fixes the cost of his material.

I also submit a table of prices for the years 1881 to 1891, inclusive, taken from a similar statement published by Justice, Bateman & Co., of Philadelphia. In this table the comparison is made between Ohio medium fleece and New Zealand crossbred, and the quotations for each grade are the average price for each year:

Comparison of prices of American and Australian scoured wools.

[Justice, Bateman & Co.'s bulletin, May 2, 1892.]

Year.	American scoured Ohio medium.	Australian scoured New Zealand crossbred.	Difference between the two prices.
1881	ᵹ0. 81½	ᵹ0. 34	ᵹ0. 47½
1882	. 76¾	. 31	. 45¾
1883	. 71½	. 26	. 45½
1884	. 66½	. 27	. 39½
1885	. 55	. 29	. 26
1886	. 60	. 31	. 29
1887	. 63½	. 33½	. 30½
1888	. 58½	. 31	. 27½
1889	. 63½	. 33	. 30½
1890	. 61½	33½	. 27½
1891	. 61½	. 34	. 27½
Average difference for the eleven years.			. 34

Justice, Bateman & Co. make the following statement in regard to the wools included in this latter table:

Both of the above grades are three-eighths or one-half blood merino. They each shrink about 40 per cent in the scouring. There are perhaps no other wools in the world so nearly alike and so suitable for a fair comparison of the European and American prices as Ohio medium and the grade of Australasian medium known as New Zealand crossbred, as they are both spun to the same numbers or counts.

The English figures given in this table are furnished by Messrs. Windeler & Co., of London, and the American figures by Messrs. Mauger & Avery.

It will be noticed that the average difference between American and English wools in this case is 34 cents a pound. Upon the basis of these comparisons it must be evident:

That the successful prosecution of wool-growing as an American industry depends upon the maintenance of a wool tariff. I know of no single instance in which protective duties have been more effectual or where the direct and positive benefits are so apparent as in the duty upon wool.

The results of this examination also establish the necessity of maintaining existing specific rates upon woolen goods, if the duty is to be maintained on wool and the business of manufacturing woolens is to be carried on in the United States.

I have elsewhere referred to the Senator's claim that labor in the United States is as cheap as anywhere in the world; but to show how far wide of the mark this statement is when applied to operatives in woolen mills, I will print in the RECORD a table of the relative wages paid.

This table furnishes the most complete and authoritative statement of relative wages in worsted mills that I know of. The rates were collected by an expert from the books of manufacturers and show that American wages are on an average more than 100 per cent higher than those in competing countries.

The Senator from Missouri was troubled with conflicting emotions when considering the case of the woolen manufacturers. After claiming that the wool duties did not benefit the farmer, he said:

> Every dollar of it—that is, the duty upon wool—has gone into the pockets of the manufacturer, and will continue to go there. * * * It is nothing but a bounty that goes to the manufacturer.

In this connection he stated that the profits of a single establishment, the Arlington Mills, had been 50 per cent in a single year; and yet in another portion of his speech he said:

> The general wool-manufacturing industry of the country has gone down. The men who are the legitimate wool manufacturers have lost money.

It may be profitable to pay some attention to the question raised by the honorable Senator in regard to the profits of woolen manufacturers, especially in view of the statements that are constantly reiterated that protective tariff benefits the few at the expense of the many, and that manufacturers are reaping enormous rewards in all protected industries. The Senator from Iowa [Mr. ALLISON] will answer in respect to the profits of the Arlington Mills, and I will invite your consideration to the report of the bureau of statistics of labor of Massachusetts for 1890, which contains an elaborate examination into the net profits of the manufacturing industries of that State. As a result of this exhaustive examination, it is shown that the average net profits in establishments producing woolen goods in Massachusetts for the year for which the statistics were obtained were 5.21 per cent of the selling price, equivalent to 5.47 per cent of the capital invested. Similar investigations in regard to the production of worsted goods showed that the net profits in this industry amounted to 2.34 per cent on the selling price, equivalent to 2.21 per cent on the capital invested.

The report of the bureau of labor statistics of Connecticut contains similar statistics in regard to the profit of woolen manufacturers in that State. This report shows that the net profits on the capital invested in 1890 were 7.57 per cent and on the value of goods manufactured 7.19 per cent. In 1889 the profits on capital were 4.27 per cent, and on the value of goods 3.43 per cent. In 1888, on capital, 4.73 per cent; on goods manufactured, 4.83 per cent. In 1887, a loss of seventeen-hundredths of 1 per cent on the capital, with a profit of two-tenths of 1 per cent on the value of goods manufactured.

These statistics prove that the average profit to the manufacturer of woolen goods for the years covered by the inquiry is not greater than the average rate of interest, and effectually dispose of the statement of the Senator from Missouri in regard to exorbitant profits of wool manufacturers. The reports alluded to contain similar statistics showing that the profits on other manufactures approximate those in woolen manufactures.

It would be perilous for the Senator from Missouri to place the various parts of his wool tariff argument in proximity.

If, as he asserts, with so much assurance in each case, (1) the cost of wool to the American woolen manufacturer is no greater than to his foreign competitor; and (2) if labor is even cheaper here than abroad; and (3) if the legitimate woolen manufacturers lose money; and (4) if the tariff on woolens is 100 per cent ad valorem, it must be evident, with annual importations of manufactures of wool valued at from forty to fifty millions of dollars, paying these high duties, that the generous foreign manufacturer pays from his own pocket the full amount of the high duty for the privilege of selling his products to the American people. The unsoundness of each of the Senator's premises, however, saves him from an embarrassing choice of absurd conclusions.

The framers of the act of 1890 were confident that the adoption of its provisions would lead to the establishment of new and the enlargement and development of old industries. Notwithstanding the fact that the elections of 1890 greatly hindered the march of improvement in this direction, the result attained has been satisfactory. Many new industries have been established which had no existence in 1890. Of these the most notable is that of the manufacture of tin plate.

No portion of the act of 1890 received such severe criticism when the measure was under discussion in Congress as the provision which levied 2.2 cents a pound duty upon importations of tin and terne plate; and the debate in regard to the wisdom of this feature of the act continues with unabated vigor. The men who were active in presenting the case in behalf of the tin-plate industry to the committees of Congress, and who have been the pioneers in its establishment, have been subjected to undeserved villification and abuse. It would appear that in the eyes of a tariff reformer, to suggest the inauguration of a new industry in the United States is a misdemeanor, and to achieve even partial success in such an enterprise is a crime for which no punishment is too severe.

None of the pioneers I have alluded to were rich men, but they were ardent, enthusiastic, and certainly deserve credit from the American people for their energy and persistence.

While the bill was under discussion, the principal objection urged against the imposition of the duty was that the industry could never be established here; it was said that the people of Wales had attained such a degree of skill and experience that it was useless to think of competing with them in a production of which they were the complete masters. It was further urged that even if the necessary skill could be secured, that the processes by which tin plates were made were so unhealthy and degrading that American workingmen never would engage in them.

These cries of the opposition have been abandoned, and from time to time new objections, each one more trivial and absurd than its predecessor, have been discovered by the political or business opponents of the tin-plate duties. Notwithstanding all the clamor and plain downright lying that has been indulged in by the men who are putting every obstacle in the way of success in the establishment of this great industry of the United States, the work of building it up has gone steadily forward. The number of pounds of tin and terne plate manufactured in each of the

727

quarters of the fiscal year, which closed on the 30th of June, 1892, was as follows:

Quarter ending—	Pounds.
September 30, 1891	826, 922
December 31, 1891	1, 409, 821
March 31, 1892	3, 004, 087
June 30, 1892	8, 225, 691

Of the 8,225,691 pounds produced in the last quarter over 5,000,000 pounds were made from black plates produced in the United States. The competent special agent of the Treasury Department who has the collection of statistics in regard to tin plates in charge, estimates in a letter which I submit and will have printed in the RECORD, that the production for the current fiscal year will be at least 100,000,000 pounds, and that by the close of the year the production will be at the annual rate of 200,000,000 pounds.

The special agent has also prepared for me a list of the twenty-six firms and corporations who have produced tin or terne plates in the last quarter, with the amount produced by each. Seven of these names appear in the list of producers for the first time, and Mr. Ayer reports that some eight or ten additional firms expect to begin the manufacture within the present quarter. Many of the names included in the list represent the strongest firms in the country, several of whom were among the most ardent opponents of the imposition of the additional duties.

There can be no doubt but that the elections of 1890 and the possibility of Democratic success in 1892 have much to do with retarding the progress of the manufacture in the United States. That this is perfectly well understood in Wales is shown by the following extracts from the Industrial World, published in Swansea, Wales, the official organ of the Welsh tin-plate workers. The extract is taken from the issue of June 10, 1892:

Do not be deceived. The victory of the Republicans at the polls means the retention of the McKinley bill, and means the rapidly accruing loss of the 80 per cent of the export American trade. Had there been no Democratic victory in 1890 the spread of the tin-plate manufacture in the United States would have been both rapid and bona fide. That victory was a stupendous shock to the Republicans, and it almost paralyzed the would-be tin-plate manufacturers of America. Nevertheless they pulled themselves together, and at once saw that they must make as brave a showing as possible in time for the double election of November, in 1892, viz, a new Congress and a

727

President. * * * They have put up, or have appeared to put up, a good many works. * * *

Now, I contend that if the masters and men had at once seen the need of a desperate fight to upset the American programme; had met together, had sunk their fierce antipathies and jealousies and had boldly agreed to divide the hardship of the struggle for a few months, a different state of things would have been in existence now, and fewer American tin-plate establishments would have seen the light. * * * Plates ought to be cheaper as November approaches and the battle begins. It is not yet too late to do something to reduce the price of plates. Put them down to 11s. per box of IC, 14 by 20, full-weight basis, Let the workmen take half pay for a few months, and turn out more. Then let the masters forego profits for the same time. The merchants will help to save the trade and their skins—depend upon that.

This discloses the state of feeling in Wales. On this side the water, unfortunately, the allies of the Welch manufacturers are numerous and boisterous. It will be a disgrace to American enterprise if the opportunity to establish this great manufacture in our midst, which is now within the reach of success, is allowed to fail.

All patriotic Americans should agree as to the benefits that would accrue from the addition of this manufacture to the catalogue of national industries.

While the Senate tariff bill of 1888 was pending in the Committee on Finance much testimony was taken in regard to the relative cost of producing tin plate in Wales and in the United States. These statements showed that the duty then asked for, would be necessary in order to thoroughly protect the American producer. For the purpose of ascertaining what changes if any had taken place in the relative cost of production, I have requested a gentleman who is thoroughly familiar with conditions on both sides of the Atlantic to furnish me a statement of the relative cost of producing tin plates at the present time. This statement, which I submit, and will have printed in the RECORD, shows the details of cost in the two countries. These figures show that the cost of making IC coke plate to-day in the United States is $5.32 per box, and in Wales $3.20 per box.

A close analysis of this table will show that the difference in cost is really a difference in the wages paid in the two countries. To substantiate this more fully, I submit and will have printed in the RECORD a table showing the wages actually paid per box in tin and black plate mills in Wales and in the United States. This table shows the actual difference in the cost of labor in the

727

production of tin plates from the bars to the finished sheet. They are the wages established by the Tin Plate Workers' Union in Wales and by the Amalgamated Association of Iron and Steel Workers in the United States, and there can be no question about their accuracy.

Statements of the relative cost of production have recently been published by Mr. J. D. Weeks in the American Manufacturer, which show the foreign cost at $2.97 and the American cost at $4.90. Mr. Weeks's figures do not allow for wastage, and are made up for Pittsburg, and show a lower cost of bars than those submitted by me, which take as a basis the cost to Eastern manufacturers. The estimated difference in cost in the two countries is practically the same in both cases and establishes the fact that existing duties are not excessive.

In order to show how completely the Welch manufacturers control the price of tin plates and how they have been accustomed to manipulate the market for their own benefit, usually at the expense of consumers in the United States, I submit herewith a statement which shows the relative price of I C coke plates and of Bessemer tin-plate bars and tin at London and Liverpool at the dates named:

	First week in—		
	September, 1890.	May, 1891.	July, 1892.
IC coke tin plate, per box	$3.41	$4.06	$3.03
Bessemer tin-plate bars, per ton	26.76	24.94	23.04
Tin, per ton	457.45	444.67	489.85

By this table it appears that while the price of IC coke tin advanced between September, 1890, and May, 1891, 65 cents a box, the price of Bessemer bars declined $1.82 per ton, and the price of pig tin declined $12.78 per ton.

With the decline which took place in bars alone between September and May, other things being equal, the price of tin plate should have declined 11 cents per box. Instead of this, there was an advance of 65 cents per box, made possible by the condition of affairs in America, the American tin-plate duties going into effect July 1, 1891; and the profits of the Welsh manufacturers were increased 76 cents per box in 1891, as compared with 1890.

40

The price of coal also declined in this period 36 cents per ton. Wages and other costs undoubtedly remained substantially unchanged, as the wages paid, union prices, in tin-plate works in Wales have not changed for fifteen years.

An equally striking exhibition is made in the comparison between May, 1891, and July, 1892. In this period the price of bars further declined $1.90 per ton, and the reduction in a box of tin plates based upon this decline should have been 12 cents a box, other things remaining equal. Instead of this, the actual decline was $1.03 per box, or a reduction in this case of the profits of the Welsh manufacturer of 91 cents per box.

It is evident from these statements that the Welsh prices are put up and down in response to existing exigencies in the United States. When the prophesies of their allies on this side of the water in regard to high prices were to be verified, prices were put up 90 cents per box in the face of a sharp decline in materials; but when American manufacturers are to be discouraged and if possible driven out of the market, on the eve of an election, the price is put down $1.03 per box.

In the absence of an American industry, American consumers are thus always at the mercy of the foreign producers. It will be noticed that with the advance in duties of 1.2 cents per pound there is a decline in the Welsh market of more 'than a cent a pound on light-weight plates, the present price of these plates being, as I have already shown, more than a dollar a box less than the price in 1891, and 3s. 6d. lower than the average price for the twelve years from 1878 to 1889, inclusive.

From this showing it is very uncertain whether any saving in cost to the American consumer would be effected by the removal of the tin-plate duties, as it would probably result in a restoration of price by the Welsh manufacturer.

When the act of 1890 was before the Senate, I expressed great confidence that within three years, if the tin-plate duties were imposed, that a considerable portion of the tin plate consumed in the United States would be of American production. I have no reason whatever to change the views then expressed. Everything that has transpired since confirms their correctness. The tin-plate industry of the United States is now an accomplished fact. But one thing is necessary for its triumphant success, and that is the maintenance of the protective duties.

The exports from Great Britain to the United States for the last four years have been as follows, amounts stated in gross tons:

	Tons.			Tons.
1889	331,673	1891		442,306
1890	296,218	1892		203,941

The exports of the last twelve months being 238,365 tons less than for the previous year; 92,277 tons less than in 1890; and 127,-732 tons less than in 1889.

Of this amount, however, it should be understood that probably about 150,000,000 pounds, or about 67,000 tons, are used in the manufacture of cans for export. On these exportations a drawback is paid to the exporter practically equal to the full amount of the duties. As long as anything like the present difference in the cost of production exists between the United States and Wales the American producers can not hope to compete for this trade; so that the portion of the market which the American producer can have any expectations of securing will be represented this year by an importation of 136,000 tons. Unless we should have a reversal of the policy of the United States growing out of the elections next November, it is entirely safe to predict that within two years from this time very much the larger part of this amount will be produced in the United States by American labor.

The Senator from Missouri, in his speech of June 28, called attention to a statement made by the Tin Plate Consumers' Association, that the present output amounted to a very small percentage of the entire consumption of the United States. If we assume the consumption of the United States for last year to be 600,-000,000 pounds, or less the amount exported, 450,000,000 pounds, we should have a domestic production, based upon the returns of the last quarter, equal to about 7 per cent of the total consumption. Considering the difficulties which the tin-plate manufacturers have had to overcome, many of them difficulties which are inherent to the introduction of any new industry, and taking into consideration the discouraging effect of the political influences to which I have referred, it seems to me that the progress

727

made is very satisfactory and will compare very favorably with the progress made at the inception of the steel rail manufacture or in the inauguration of any of the other great branches of the iron and steel industry.

Another point which was made by the Senator from Missouri finds a place in the speech of every opponent of tin-plate duties. It is the claim, which has often been controverted, that the movement to put an additional duty upon tin-plate originated with the galvanized sheet-iron manufacturers of Pittsburg, whose sole object was to advance the price of their own product and prevent the competition that might arise from the use of tin-plate for roofing purposes. It is further claimed in this connection that these gentlemen had no idea of establishing the tin-plate manufacture in the United States, and that no serious attempt in that direction is now being made.

In proof of their alleged purpose, the Senator from Missouri claims that an advance of 1 cent per pound in the price of galvanized sheet iron followed closely upon the imposition of the additional tin-plate duties of 1.2 cents per pound. The following list of prices of galvanized sheet iron, No. 24 gauge, for each of the years from 1888 to 1892, inclusive, has been furnished me by the McDaniel & Harvey Company, one of the largest manufacturers of galvanized sheet iron in the country.

Average price of galvanized sheet iron, No. 24 gauge.
[The same proportion holds good for all other gauges.]

Year.	List price per pound.	Discount.	Net price per pound.
	Cents.		Cents.
1888	13	65 and 5 per cent	4.32½
1889	13	67½ and 2 per cent	4.12
1890	13	67½ per cent	4.22½
1891	13	67½ and 5 per cent	4.01½
1892 (up to July)	14	70 and 10 per cent	3.78

This statement shows that while the list price was advanced 1 cent per pound, as claimed, that the discounts from this list were simultaneously increased from 67½ and 5 per cent to 70 and 10 per cent, resulting in a net reduction instead of an increase in price. The table submitted shows a gradual decline in price from 1888 up to the present time. I will print in the RECORD the letter of the company referred to transmitting the table.

It disproves in every respect the other allegations contained in the statement of the Senator from Missouri.

There is another allegation made by the critics of the tin-plate duty which perhaps should be noticed. It is that a considerable portion of the tin plate produced here is manufactured from imported black plates. Fortunately, however, the statistics of production for the quarter just closed state the proportions made from foreign and domestic plates, and establishes the inaccuracy of the claim. This allegation was based upon certain comparative statistics of the importation of rolled sheets. This comparison does not take into account, however, the amount of sheets thinner than No. 25, wire gauge, that were imported prior to October, 1890, as taggers' iron. Most of the thin black sheets imported under the old tariff law were imported as taggers' iron, whatever might have been their character, on account of the lower rate of duty on this description. Importations under this classification were more than 12,000,000 pounds in 1889.

Under the tariff act of 1883 the cotton-ties used in the United States were imported. Since the enactment of existing law the American manufacturer of cotton-ties has supplied the entire demand, and they are sold at a lower cost to the consumer. The imposition of adequate protective duties upon lace window-curtains, silk and mohair plushes, pearl buttons, and many other articles has transferred important industries to the United States.

We are now producing a large variety of the finer and more expensive manufactures of cotton, wool, and iron, all of which were imported prior to 1890. Manufacturers are enlarging their capacity for production, and in every branch of industry the greatest activity prevails. Some manufactures, notably that of woolen goods, were dull and lifeless for a considerable period subsequent to the adoption of the act on account of excessive competition with the enormous amounts of foreign goods that had been imported in anticipation of an advance of duties and prices. These stocks have been largely disposed of.

The condition of the woolen industry is shown by the following extract from the Boston Herald, the leading tariff-reform newspaper in the country, under date of July 15, 1892:

727

Where is the idle woolen mill to-day? Indeed there is none, or the number is so few that they are not worth counting. Not only is the great majority of the woolen mills employed, but many of the manufacturers are contemplating enlargements and improvements, or such enlargements and improvements are already begun. What does this all mean? It means simply the greatest consumption of wool that the country has known for years.

In the iron and steel industry the work of expansion is going on, but prices are very low and profits small.

A comparison of the value of dutiable merchandise imported in 1892 with the importation of the same articles in 1889 will furnish an indication of the extent to which the market of the American producer has been enlarged by the direct operations of the act of 1890.

The importations of these articles in 1889 amounted in value to $389,000,000, and in 1892 to $363,500,000, or a decline in three years of $25,350,000. If the value of the imported articles of this class had increased at the same ratio with the increase in the value of all importations, the importations in 1892 would have been $50,-000,000 greater than in 1889, instead of $25,500,000 less. It would appear from this comparison that articles of the foreign value of at least $75,000,000, were produced in the United States in the fiscal year 1892, which, if it had not been for the adoption of the act of 1890, would have been imported. If we add a portion of average rate of duty to this sum we should have a value of domestic production redeemed from foreign competitors of at least $100,000,000. This production would furnish employment to 200,000 people and support nearly a million. All of this is of course an addition to the natural growth of our industries.

Perhaps the most extraordinary statement made in either of the Senator's speeches is the following:

The wool manufacture of the United States is in the hands of a trust.

This allegation, that there is a trust which controls the manufacture of woolens, is repeated by the Senator from Missouri several times in the course of his argument.

It is the climax of absurdity to say that the business of woolen manufacturing in the United States is or ever has been controlled to any extent by a trust. No such trust or even a combination of any kind has ever existed. It would be quite impossible to make any combination that would or could control prices or production of woolen goods, as the number of establishments is so great, and the styles manufactured of such infinite variety.

It is difficult to conceive how the Senator from Missouri could have been misled into making this statement. I have never seen the allegation anywhere else; and yet his objections to the wool and woolen duties rest largely upon the positive statement of the existence of such a trust.

But the Senator from Missouri does not stop with the wool manufacturers' trust. He presented to the Senate and had printed in the RECORD on the 28th of June an additional list of so-called tariff trusts, one hundred in number. These trusts, the Senator from Missouri claimed, were the necessary results of our recent tariff legislation, and he insists that by their operation competition had been stifled and prices advanced. The Senator was gracious enough to admit that, "If there were no trusts, and factories were increased in any department of industry in the United States, the competition between manufacturers would bring down the prices;" but he assumes "that this legitimate result is never allowed to obtain, because as soon as the manufacturers secure the tariff duty, they get together to destroy the competition and form combinations."

For the purpose of ascertaining the truth in regard to these alleged trusts, whose imaginary history covers more than twenty pages of the CONGRESSIONAL RECORD, I addressed a letter to at least one well-known manufacturer connected with each of the principal industries that were included in the list. I submit and will have printed in the RECORD a copy of my letter of inquiry, and of the replies received. No attempt was made to secure replies in regard to industries of no special commercial importance, or where the nature of the manufacture was such as to preclude the possibility of a combination to control prices and production.

These classes, twelve in number, include brooms, burial caskets, skewers, snaths, vapor stoves, umbrellas, borax, pitch, sponges, teazles, and trunks. There is another class of which no replies were requested, but where the existence of combinations that control production and prices to a greater or less extant is well known; and still another, to whom the letter of in-

727

quiry was sent, but who failed to respond. Both these latter classes, eight in number, include celluloid, matches, oatmeal, rubber gossamers, smelters, sugar, stove boards, and spool bobbin and shuttle. As there is no duty on anthracite coal I did not take the trouble to investigate the so-called anthracite coal trust.

The representatives of seventy-nine industries replied to my letter of inquiry. Of these the representatives of seventy-two deny in the most emphatic manner the existence of any trust in the industries with which they are connected. Most of them, as will be seen by an examination of the letters, denying in detail all the statements published by the Senator from Missouri. Seven of the parties denied the existence of a trust, but admitted in a qualified way the existence of combinations which were intended to be more or less effective in controlling prices.

It appears from the answers received that in none of the industries reported upon is there a trust in existence, or even a combination created with a view to control prices and production, whose creation was the result of the tariff or of protective duties, and it does not appear that any of the small number of existing combinations has had the effect to increase the cost of the articles manufactured to consumers.

The complete and crushing character of the denials can only be appreciated by a careful examination of the letters themselves. I would be glad, if time permitted, to read them all in the presence of the Senate. I will ask to have a few read by the Secretary to indicate the character of the whole.

I feel that I owe you an apology for taking the time of the Senate in the extended examination of Mr. WARNER'S list of socalled trusts. The statement as a whole bore upon its face convincing evidence of its unreliable character. It is simply a collection of miserable libels on the men who control and conduct the great business enterprises of the country. I am inclined to think that the time spent in exposing its true character has been wasted, as I can not believe that the intelligent people of any community would give credence to such preposterous statements.

It is very evident, however, from the declarations of the Senator from Missouri that this paper is to be printed and circulated in large numbers throughout the country in the approaching campaign, and for this reason I have been induced to place the facts upon the public records, where they can be known and read of all men.

I have attempted to answer all the objections to the act of 1890 that have been brought to my attention; but I have no idea that the work of the friends of protection in this direction is ended, as the crop of such misrepresentations is perennial.

There is no limit to the ingenuity or resources of the persons employed in manufacturing statistics for the purpose of breaking down the protective system.

There has been heretofore, however, no halting or turning aside in the triumphal march of the American people to industrial success and independence by reason of the fabrications' prophesies, or hysterical cries of professional reformers; and as I have unbounded faith in the brave and vigorous men, the best fruits of American civilization, who are now leading the way to greater achievements, I do not believe that their progress in the future will be retarded by those who stand by the wayside and make faces at the moving column.

There is no permanent place in American politics for a party that bases its claims for popular support on the failures and disappointment of the people.

The purpose of the act of 1890, as repeatedly stated by its advocates on this floor, was to provide for the better security and the greater development of American industries and to maintain the high level of wages then existing in the United States. The claims and expectations of the framers of the measure have been more than realized. Through its various provisions it has enlarged the markets, both foreign and domestic, of American producers. It has secured the establishment of new industries and given vitality and expansion to old ones.

It has quickened the pulsations of trade, given a new impetus to agriculture as well as to manufactures and commerce. By its revival of activities in every direction it has given profitable employment and certainty of earnings to all classes of the people. It has directed American enterprise into new channels and given wider scope to the genius of American inventors. It has afforded

727

the opportunity for production in the United States of all the finer and more difficult manufactures in every branch, industries which will demand from our artisans and skilled workmen greater artistic taste and a higher mental development.

The beneficial effect which the entrance upon these new and broader industrial fields will have in quickening the national life and broadening the national experience can not be measured by the sum which the establishment of these industries will add to the national income.

The declared purpose of the Democratic party to repeal this act immediately upon their return to power is certain to provoke a lively opposition to their political restoration.

We can await the result of this contest with calm confidence. The plain people of the United States have too much good sense and discernment to mistake pretentious platitudes for philosophy. They are not likely to exchange the certainty of satisfactory earnings and savings, of constant employment and comfortable homes, for Democratic promises of a millennium that is to follow revolution. These promises are but the shadows of the unknown for which an intelligent people will not surrender the substance of a present and abundant prosperity.

727

O

www.ingramcontent.com/pod-product-compliance
Lightning Source LLC
Chambersburg PA
CBHW032122080426
42733CB00008B/1026